BETTI

FOOTBALL SOCCER

OVER 0,5

SECOND HALF

"Better an egg Today or the Hen Tomorrow?"

STEP-BY-STEP GUIDE TO

"ONE GOAL PAY 2 HALF STRATEGY"

www.alexbettin.com

INDEX

Disclaimer

GAMBLING IS FORBIDDEN TO UNDERAGE AND IT CAN CREATE PATHOLOGICAL ADDICTION AND GAMBLING DISORDERS

Introduction

If you have decided to read this book, you have surely guessed the potential of this Strategy, which, if you apply it with constancy and confidence, will allow you to accumulate significant capital in the long term.

Yes, because this new Strategy I've been testing for over a year is a valid form of LONG-TERM INVESTMENT.

Not only that, applied in combination with my other Strategies (from the most aggressive to the most conservative ones) will allow you always to have a treasure to reinvest.

After three years of active betting and studying the different strategies, I can say with certainty that not every day is the same as the others, and not every day do we need the same emotions.

Add also that the schedules change daily, and here is why this Strategy I called "No Stress" was born.

I can consider this Strategy, to all intents and purposes, THE ULTIMATE STRATEGY, the one that allows you to recover (should you have made a few missteps), which will enable you to accumulate (if your need is to grow your capital constantly) the one that allows you to create money from money (to be able to risk a little more with more aggressive Strategies.)

What you will find in this guidebook is the Strategy of Strategies, the most "performing" from an operational point of view and the one that, in the long run, allows great economic satisfaction (even if from an emotional point of view, it lacks little adrenaline).

If you have the patience to learn and follow me, I'm sure the day will come when you can use all my strategies, dosing them according to the schedules and dividing your budget into a more aggressive and long-term Strategy.

I wish you a good reading, and I invite you to view my other books, which you will find summarized at the end of this publication.

Happy Bet Simple!

Do you want to have Fun or Earn?

In almost all my publications, this is a fundamental theme. I have quoted it in another form, "Do you want to earn or be right" but the substance does not change.

Getting a prediction right generates a release of dopamine that makes us euphoric and happy. On the one hand, we were right, and on the other, we gained thanks and this.

However, I ask you how often you have been in a "roller coaster" situation. How much is it?

How many times has the account inflated and then deflated at double speed due to Bets made on the sensations of the moment?

To overcome this, you can undoubtedly rely on the Money Management techniques in my last two books dedicated to my strategies.

However, there is still another way that you could follow to reach the TOP of long-term results.

Because that's what you want, right? You want to earn something daily to have an extra nest egg at the end of the month, right? I'm sure that's the case and that many of you already manage to achieve this result constantly, but there are certainly others who, for various reasons, have a "need" for adrenaline, which is an "expensive" need.

Don't worry; I have the solution, it took me a long time to convince myself, but today I'm sure of it, and I'm ready to almost "guarantee" it. I've decided to put it in black and white now that I'm sure of it.

The Strategy that we will see shortly is something "crazy" enough to guarantee the right amount of "adrenaline," but at the same time "safe," I feel I can say it. Do the test for 30/60 days with a tiny budget and check at the end what % of profit it brought you. Then replace the numbers with more "important" digits, and I'm sure a smile will break out on your face from side to side...

Introduction to Strategy

Anyone who has known me for a long time and is familiar with my operational strategies knows that I have evolved in various directions over the past two years. My BEST SELLER with which this splendid project started is the book "Sports Betting Over 0.5 - Complete Guide to the ONE GOAL PAY Strategy".

It all started from here, a safe and conservative strategy with great debate in the past on social networks. Thanks to my Challenge Live on my website, www.alexbettin.com, the discussion ended thanks to the publicly obtained results. From this Strategy, I built the following ones working on increasingly aggressive odds getting excellent results and great "adrenaline."

You know it well, this pace is not sustainable forever, I'm also starting to get old, and I also have to pay attention to my health, physical and mental.

From this need, I started from the "fundamentals," from the beginning of my career, from the Over 0.5 Strategy, but looking for mediation on the "share" value.

I already expect new criticisms and discussions but fear nothing and am ready for a NEW LIVE CHALLENGE!

Before starting, however, I want to re-propose one of the FUNDAMENTAL chapters of my first book because I consider it a sort of COMMANDMENT of Betting, and I hope you will agree too.

The Bet of Live Betting

Living on sports betting is the aspiration of many people, just as it was fashionable a few years ago to be able to live on Online Trading.

The two things are pretty similar; I went through a phase in which I tried to use Online Trading to achieve financial freedom.

Even in the world of sports betting and Online Trading, a good basic strategy is needed to have "total confidence" and a lot of knowledge of the leagues (or reference markets).
The choice of the Broker platform (in the case of sports betting, the Bookmaker platform) should not be underestimated. It may seem superficial, but having faith in your Bookmaker and familiarizing yourself with its platform is vital.

Knowing the response times during the betting phase, having confidence in the deposit-withdrawal circuit, and having serenity about adequate customer support are the reasons why I always suggest you use only one Bookmaker.

I have found all this in BET365, but this does not mean other bookmakers are not up to the task. You evaluate one Bookmaker and another and choose the more "functional" to your operations and your times.

Is this enough to earn constantly from sports betting? And above all, is all this enough to transform this passion into a real job with a monthly salary? Certainly not, at least in my experience.

There is a strong determining element not only in the world of betting but in life itself, and it is the Mindset. Being able to live (or perhaps better, to live) with the emotional stress of the world of sports betting is not for everyone.

Your mind and solar plexus are always stimulated and tense, even in the face of the most obvious bets. Often at the end of a live match, it seems to you that you have played the game yourself. Holding the tension before, during, and after the bet is essential to make a living from this passion.

Also, knowing your tolerance to the loss of money is another element that will determine your ability or otherwise to operate in this activity. A good strategy, especially at the beginning, to "test" your loss tolerance threshold is to start with the minimum bet the broker allows and double it in the following 6/7 chances. Although you will almost certainly lose some money this way, you can quickly figure out what is causing you too much emotional tension.

Think of it as an initial investment that will save you terrible suffering in the future. Once you find your threshold, stay €10 below it for at least a year. You can retest the situation the following year and evaluate if it has risen.

We have just mentioned two essential words which, if fully understood, will make the difference between who will succeed and who will not: "Mindset" and "Investment."

Living on sports bets today is only possible in one way; you must be willing to evolve your Mindset. We are no longer talking about sports betting but about investing in sporting events. It may seem trivial, but your terminology acts immediately on the mind and, consequently, on the behavior.

To make a living from sports betting, you need to start an investment company in sports events. You are beginning a real entrepreneurial activity. If you think about any project, even online, you will need a budget, you will have to set long and short-term goals, you will have to study the reference market and be able to evaluate the risk/return of your investments, you will have to give yourself working hours and moments of "detachment" and why not, a specific physical place in which to operate.

The advantages of succeeding in this activity are enormous, starting from the earnings on which YOU WILL NOT PAY A CENT IN TAXES! You already knew that.

If you operate on Bookmakers regulated in our country, taxes are paid at source by the Bookmakers themselves.

"Find me another LEGAL but untaxed source of income!"

How the Strategy Works

I have already told you the reason for this new strategy, but another reason makes it "attractive."

Over the last year, I have noticed some changes in my attitude toward football sports matches. Many teams attack their opponents in the first minutes of matches, making it difficult to bet on big odds in the first half. The advent of playing time options certainly offers an additional possibility of earning but requires large budgets to be able to follow the climbs.

The option remains (which is very valid in many leagues) to bet on the first-half goal in the very last minutes (between the 35th and 40th minute), with odds ranging between 3 and 4.

At the end of the book, I "give" you a list of championships in which the percentage of wins with this technique reaches even 70/75%. It can therefore be an excellent complementary strategy that requires meager budgets (even with €1 per stake, good results can be obtained in the long run) and which I frequently use with my subscribers to Live signals. If you want to enter for a free trial period, you can find all the information on my website www.alexbettin.com

We said several things have changed, but one has remained the same: the percentage of goals scored in the second half is always higher than in the first half. It is no coincidence that the odds are much less "inviting" than those proposed in the early days.

This consolidated statistic, therefore, offers the right pillar on which to build a strategy.

The doubts of many remain concerning the low odds, but compared to my classic Over 0.5

Strategy, albeit still very valid, especially in the South American championships), it allows you to operate at reasonable odds, which, combined with the high percentage of times in which verify a goal in the second half, makes everything almost foolproof (at least in the long run).

ATTENTION: I'm not saying to apply this strategy randomly on the schedule; mind you, there are event selection rules exactly like for my Over 0.5 Strategy that I will show you in the Guide section of this book.

Operations

You should have understood how it works by now, but let's do a p√≤ of order and some live examples.

As I told you, this new Strategy is based on two pillars:

THE GOALS IN THE SECOND HALF ARE GREATER THAN THE GOALS ACCOMPLISHED IN THE FIRST HALF

SCORING A GOAL IN THE SECOND HALF OF A MATCH HAS A PERCENTAGE OF CLOSE TO 80%*

*(In selected matches with my Strategy)

Starting from these two "assumptions," the operational Strategy is straightforward. For the daily activities and the management of the Stakes, I avail myself of the help of the MASANIELLO System.

Below you will find MY configuration.

Step	Data	Partita	Segno	Quota	Esito	Giocata	Vincita	Cassa	Stato
0	Data	Partita						509.01 €	
1				1,30	Vinto	79 €	102.7 €	532.71 €	In corso
2				1,35	Vinto	58 €	85 €	549.71 €	In corso
3				1,25		53 €			
4				1,25					
5				1,25					
6				1,25					
7				1,25					
8				1,25					

Target: 7 Vinte — Quota riferimento: 1.25 — Quota media: 1.26

My configuration in summary includes:

1- Budget (in my case €500, but it can be any amount)

2- Total Number of Events (usually I work with ten events at a time)

3- The average odds on which I bet (in my case, it is 1.25 and usually represents the odds in effect 5/8 minutes after the start of the 2nd half)

4- Number of target events to win (in my case, seven and therefore a target of 70% of wins and below that 80/85% mentioned above)

The final result we will obtain at the end of the seven wins will be a 15% increase in the Budget. Whatever the starting Budget value, we are talking about a 15% gain on a case with a positive outcome in 80/85%*, which can potentially be obtained daily (based on the number of selected events available). Do you calculate the potentially monthly earnings?

IF IT NEVER FAILED ONE DAY (statistically impossible), that starting €500 reinvested every day, including earnings, would become €153,000.

If, on the other hand, I kept the Budget fixed every day by replicating the same system every day, I would earn €2,210, a TAX-FREE SALARY.

*(In selected matches with my Strategy)

Warning Notes

Now that I have shown you the potential of this Strategy and why I consider it the IDEAL Strategy to accumulate constant earnings over time, let me bring you some notes of Attention with which to approach and which must be respected to avoid ruining the beauty it offers.

1- BE TRUE TO THE STRATEGY

Too often, we switch from one Strategy to another, not giving it time to produce results. So if. You decide to leave, do it, and don't be scared of a possible loss (and not even in front of two)

2- DON'T BE IMPATIENT

When you are ready to enter, but the quota has not yet reached the threshold you have defined,

DO NOT RETURN if they score earlier. Move on to the next. In the long run, the Strategy will work.

3- DO NOT PLAY ON 2/+ SIMULTANEOUS EVENTS

If you have two "useful" events, DO NOT enter simultaneously; choose which one to enter first and wait for the win. If the second event still hasn't scored a goal at the end of the first, you can enter; otherwise, wait for the next one.

4- DO NOT USE THE STRATEGY WITH MINUTES OR MULTIPLES

It is not recommended to combine events in multiples or operate by playing time; you should have huge budgets to be able to do it

5-DON'T USE THE STRATEGY IN THE FIRST TIMES

Although simple, DO NOT apply this Strategy to the first half, making you greedy by the odds.

For the first few times, follow what is explained in my book: Over 05 Strategy at High Altitude, which you can find on Amazon or my website, www.alexbettin.com, or enter my LIVE Channel where I report in real time the moments of entry to the first final time. (or take advantage of the championship list at the end of this book)

This Strategy is certainly not very "adrenaline" and is 100% focused on earnings accumulation. So beware of possible moments of boredom that can be "lethal" for your earnings. DON'T HUNT for more LIVE events to kill boredom and stick to selected events.

If you are subscribed to any prediction channel, LOG OUT for at least a month, so you don't have any temptations or doubts about your selection. Following the instructions in the Guide on the following pages, you should have a winning list in hand daily.

Happy Bet Simple!

STEP-BY-STEP GUIDE:
"EVENT SELECTION"

Event Selection

As with the Over 0.5 ONE GOAL PAY Strategy, the correct selection of Events is the basis of the results.

The first ideal thing to do is identify a list of teams that have the characteristic of having an average game goal of at least "3".

To do this, the site (or the App) of

www.diretta.it

I recommend joining the site to take full advantage of the match selection and monitoring services.

Once registered, you can enter up to 100 teams. "Favorites"; in this way, you will find all the scheduled events every day in the dedicated section.

To identify the 100 teams to be monitored for the application of the Strategy, the first step that needs to be done is to identify the teams with an average goal equal to or greater than "3" for the various leagues.

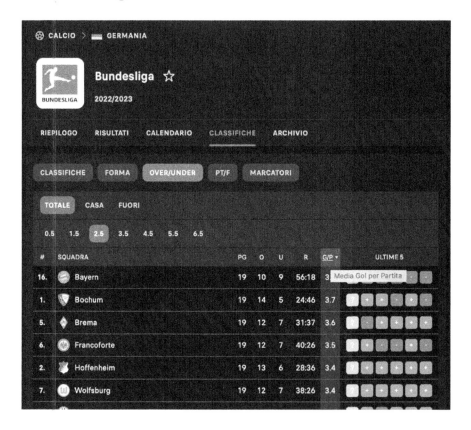

As shown in the picture above, the steps to do are:

- Choose the Championship (in this case, BUNDELIGA)

- Click on Standings and check that at least ten games have been played

- Click on the "Over/Under" selection and then the "G/P" item, which identifies the average match goals per team.

- All teams with an average Goal equal to or greater than "3" are valid for the Strategy. To add them to your favorites, click on the team name and select "star."

Once this step has been taken and the limit of 100 teams has been reached, you will automatically find in the "Favourites" section at the top left the list of all the events in which the 100 teams will be involved in the coming days and weeks.

The first important step is done. From now on, you will ONLY watch and operate these teams; everything else is a DISTRACTION.

I'm sure you're wondering what a team's goal average has to do with the fact that we'll bet on a goal in the second half now we get there.

The most important job will be skimming the favorite events every day (preferably in the morning) or the evening of the next day.

It is said that a team with an average goal equal to or greater than "3" scores at least one goal every time it plays.

Understanding how he behaves and the characteristics of the opposing team is a crucial element to evaluate.

For each event, it is necessary to enter the "Head to Head" section to understand how often the two teams score in the second half and, above all, if they score more goals in the second half or in the first.

To do this, click on the match, and in the Head/Head section, check the individual matches played in the last period.

ATTENTION: In the last period, not last year or two years before. Teams change over time!

If the numbers are on the side of Strategy (most of the goals are scored in the second half by both teams, the last few games have started with at least three goals, and even the direct matches in the past have offered a good number of goals per game), then it is "good."

Otherwise, if we talk about a favorite team, the bet on that match is discarded.

In the photo on the previous page, the favorite team was Central Coast, and the parameters of today's match entirely fell within those of the Strategy.

She was selected and this was the result.

By following these simple steps, you will automatically have a list of events every day that you will only have to skim. If you also download the Diretta. it App, you will receive match alerts in real-time.

At this point, all you need is to wait for the end of the first half and check some statistics in the interval to reinforce the idea of the possibility of a next goal in the second half or not.

Once confirmed, check the next goal odds and evaluate whether to enter immediately at odds of less than 1.25 (because you expect a flash goal as it has already occurred in the past) or let the second half of the match begin and wait for developments quote.

I hope I was clear and exhaustive in explaining the steps to do. If you have any doubts, you can contact me at the addresses you find at the end of the book in the "Author Information" section or go to the website www.alexbettin.com

and book a live coach remotely (just for those who have purchased this book, I have decided to add two discount codes for coaching and subscription to the live channel on the last page.

Before leaving you, I would like to thank you for coming this far; I truly hope that this new Strategy can be a turning point for you as it has been and still is for me.

A hug

Happy Bet Simple

Conclusions

If you've come this far, I want to thank you very much for the time you dedicated to me; I hope you could have perceived my enthusiasm for this activity and the great results that can be achieved with the right strategy.

As I have already told you previously, I am not a professional in the sector, and this publication does not in any way want to be an instigation to start this business.

All my services aim to demonstrate that it is possible to earn a salary from sports betting as long as you have a solid strategy, a very disciplined approach, and Mindset. I conclude by indicating in the next chapter all my references and ways to follow me, and I hope soon to have you in my private community and keep my promise:

Championships valid for Over close to the term 1 TIME:

1. Gambia
2. Brasile
3. Iran
4. Siria
5. Kuwait

Bibliography Update 2023

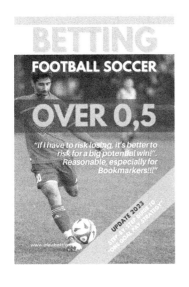

Betting Football Soccer OVER 05

Over 05 Match/Prematch

Stake: Medium/High

Betting Football Soccer OVER HT ADRENALIVE

Over Half Time Strategy high Bet Odds.

Stake: Medium/Low

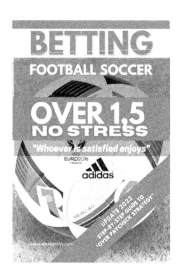

Betting Football Soccer OVER 1,5 NO STRESS

Over 1,5 Strategy Live/Prematch

Stake: Medium/Medium-High

Betting Football Soccer BETTING MONEY MANAGEMENT VOL1

A complete Guide to Budget Money Management in Sports Betting

Betting Football Soccer BETTING MONEY MANAGEMENT VOL2

A complete Guide to Budget Money Management in my Live Bot Alerts.

File Excel INCLUDED for FREE

About the Author

My name is Alex, and I have been a sports betting strategy enthusiast for years.

After years of study and attempts in the field, I have developed several profitable Strategies that have been paying me a monthly tax-free salary for the past one and a half years!*

* Possible ONLY with ADM Bookmakers recognized in ITALY

On my website, www.alexbettin.com, or in the main online and offline bookstores, you can find the strategy that best suits your characteristics among my publications, without forgetting my latest work dedicated to Budget Management in Sports Betting.

It's all-natural and demonstrated daily and since I know how much fake information passes daily on YouTube and the net, I have decided to make each step as transparent as possible.

If you want to know better and learn personally how I select the events according to my strategies, you can contact me by email at: betdamale74@gmail.com or visit my website: www.alexbettin.com.

On my site, you will find all the articles on predictions, outcomes, the Challenge, and paid services with which you too can learn about this strategy and put it into practice independently.

At this point, I close by thanking you again for reading my book, and I hope you can make a dream come true as I did.

BETTING
FOOTBALL SOCCER
OVER 0,5
SECOND HALF

"Better an egg Today or the Hen Tomorrow?"

STEP-BY-STEP GUIDE TO

"ONE GOAL PAY 2 HALF STRATEGY"

www.alexbettin.com

Printed in Great Britain
by Amazon